Going Gentle

Fiona Owen

Gomer

Published in 2007 by Gomer Press, Llandysul,
Ceredigion SA44 4JL

ISBN 978 1 84323 818 8
A CIP record for this title is available from the British Library.

This book is published with the financial support of the
Welsh Books Council.

Printed and bound in Wales at
Gomer Press, Llandysul, Ceredigion

It is the intimate, never the general, that is teacherly.

Mary Oliver

CONTENTS

Walk

I am learning to walk
with my centre pitched low
so I am closer
to the ground.

In this way
it's my body that leads
that place below the navel,
some kind of meridian
power point.

This is how Tao men walked
the thousand-mile journey.

My walk is to the post office with my dog
but a voyage is a voyage.

I have found that my habit
learned over years
has been to lead with the head.

All that time spent
straining forward
has given me a cricked neck.

First there was a mountain
then there wasn't
then there was:
I am relearning a walk
that will take me to
the rest of my life −

Door

(For Mandy)

You will not find the boundaries of psyche
by travelling in any direction, so deep
is the measure of it
                        HERACLITUS

I tell you about the door I found
in my *self* – creaked it open thinking blood bowels
the usual pulsing matter
stepped onto the sill it was a *precipice*
space yawning around me no edges
my head reeled a moment of vertigo
but then I let go free fall to nowhere
nothing to hurt no landing to make
stars could tumble in worlds
so much inside this one small woman's body

'I've just been out for a lovely walk'

(For Jeremy Hilton, in autumn)

Your words take me
over the hills, to where
a green, soft heart
beats among the hedgerows.
I see you on a lane,
its surface a sheen
of sun–after–rain.
You stride along, hands in your pockets,
the season's fire on your face.
Over stiles, across plough,
you are deep in the presence
of breath. The wind has turned –
winter's harbinger – and we are not short
of news that chills. But a *lovely walk*
among crisping leaves and haw berries hanging
will always quicken me, even
in the twenty-first century.

Positioning

Yeah is what we had and no we never knew
GRANDADDY

Here I am, on my blue chair,
at the table where the window
looks out across the garden,
to the lake and the sea beyond.

The magazine beside me
reports Arctic glaciers diluting
the Atlantic as they melt.

The gulf stream is changing.
Climate could flip and this scene
outside the window where the elder
is in first leaf and the crocuses litter the lawn

would all become white: the sand-dunes, white;
the rooftops of Bryn Owain, white; Rhosneigr, white;
the lake a frozen slab, white; the garden
where our young trees are, white; field, white;
all Wales, all Europe, all all white.

An age of ice to snap off our fingers and toes.

But I lift my eyes and there you are,
in your dad's old checked shirt
mowing the long over-wintered grass
red sunshine flecking your hair
and green, green everywhere.

Clearing

The greatest gift is what the river has taught her —
to be silent, and to listen

SUZY GABLIK

She has come again to the river.
It is November and the forecast,
like the sky, says *snow*. She has the day
before her. She takes in her hand a stone
from the riverbank and offers it a silent prayer.
Then she pulls her beret down over her ears
and casts her eyes along the river. The water
flows where it can around the sofa
and supermarket trolley, bearing slowly along
fast-food debris, cardboard boxes, tin cans.
She puts on a pair of thermal, and then rubber,
gloves, shakes out her first bin bag and begins.

She works for six hours.

Condoms. Newspaper. An old hairbrush.
A baby's cot. A curtain rail. Oil cans.
Some kind of car engine that will need a winch.
And bottles, most of them broken.

When it begins to snow — feathery, falling soft
on scrubby branches, the sofa, her quilted coat —
she pauses to listen: all sounds are closer now.

It is not cold enough yet to freeze the river.
But her feet are numb in their three pairs of socks
and their Wellington boots. Over the footbridge
that spans the roadside and park, people walk —
with their dogs; alone; in pairs; in huddles.

Once, a boy threw over the side a drinks can:
it splashed just yards ahead of her. She called to him:
'You've dropped your tin.'

He turned back, saw her standing there in the river,
holding her bin bag, the water around her ankles,
and came back to lean over the rail. A second boy
swigged the last of his coke and, holding it for a moment
between thumb and forefinger, dropped the can at her feet
so that it bounced a little on the filmy surface of the water.
'Whoops,' he said, his eyebrows angling like a clown's.
And the two boys hung there, surveying her, while she
struggled with her own turbulence. Fearing words, she
instead bent before them and placed the cans
into her bag, and moved on.

It is not difficult for her to imagine the river
as a vein running through her own body.
She is blood-clearing. She is purifying
her own fluids. She is increasing healthy flow
so that the body may thrive again.

The snow sanctifies every turn of this waterway,
every blade of spiky grass, every boulder. Even the sofa –
its rotting base, its faded beige upholstery – is adorned
with a white sprinkling along its arms and headrest.
It tempts her to sit, mid-stream, as the twilight deepens
and listen to the sound of snow falling.

Too dark now. She is on her way home.
Her feet squeak in the snow as she walks
and her thoughts are ahead of her: make tea
in the pot, eat hot potato and gingerbread,
lie in a bath of suds for an hour.

She thinks of the sofa, a defunct thing
dumped in the shallows of the river.
She tries to picture the family who owned it
tipping it down the bank and watching it tumble
and she wonders whether anything stirred
within them as they drove off, their sofa
abandoned there in the river.

The heart goes through periods of sinking
but that is never the time to stop.
It is the time to sing.

The Sycamores

All day, I heard an angel crying:
'Hurt not the trees'
CHARLOTTE MEW

It's a similar day –
damp drizzle,
almost May
and the men have come
to cut the sycamores.

It is ridiculous –
sentimental –
in the twenty-first century
to be this heart-wrought
for the sake of a tree,
for some boughs and branches,
height, taken -

yet your angel,
and her plea,
hangs round me
this morning.

These are not great plane trees.
They are only common sycamores,
indigenous to this island.

But they line the lane
and the wind swishes their leaves
and my heart beats in these
in the sun, in the rains.

The men
hang,
like acrobats,

among the branches,
in harnesses.
They are climbers
and abseilers.
Their chainsaws
are scalpel instruments.
There are no 'whoops' and 'whoas',
just the professional drone
as a bough
goes,
some thumps,
the engine-sound of the shredder.

No one to blame for this.
Not the neighbour who complained
that the leaves shade the garden in summer,
untidy the garden in autumn.

Not the electricity company
whose cable is strung
between poles between trees.

Not the council.

Not the men.

But –
will trees ever be left
to grow tall
again?

The poetry professor queries his student

'Why do you write so many doggy poems
when there are such human issues in the world,
when you could interview your own
father about when he found himself hurled
into battle in World War Two and had
to first shoot one of the Germans dead?
Choosing dogs to write about is bad
judgement. It shows your head
is in the fluffy clouds.'
                              'I saw a dog
shot in the face and left to die in the road.
I was twelve. I soothed its shuddering God-
forsakenness and tasted the first unfold –
ing of life's bigger themes. Dogs and men
and tender hearts, easily broken.

To Do This Thing

To do this to such a thing
that was, this morning, so fine a thing,
so red and real a thing, so running free
a thing;
         to do this thing to such a thing
so that now, this evening, it is no more
a thing than a mud-mangled thing,
bedraggled thing, its eyes popped out
as if on springs, a cartoon thing, a wrecked
and torn and bone-broken thing, its entrails
trailing as the thing is held up, bowel hanging
out like a string of chipolata things.
                  From a sunning itself thing,
russet light-catching thing, young-rearing thing,
to a red running thing, over-blown, worn down,
chased-to-ground thing.

Eyes on stalks.   Heart thrown to the dogs.

Prey Brought Down

And he let fly an arrow.
And it entered the side of the gazelle.
And she fell in the dust.
And she swung her head towards him.
And her wild bewilderment blazed.
And the man bounded towards her.
And the thing in her side was not enough
to kill her. She must wait further moments
for the series of blows. And her herd
a last sound of thunder escaping.

August Caterpillar

I stand by the apple tree,
my attention caught
by a big fly and a caterpillar
sharing the same leaf.

They are both
steady still.

Waiting, I wonder: who will move first?

It is the caterpillar.

It raises a face
with fringed eyes.

It has a yellow stripe
down its inch-long body.

The caterpillar sways
its head
left then right.

It curls into a question.

The fly
also
has a face
and eyes

but its dark
stillness
seems suddenly
ominous.

I regard again
the caterpillar.

How tender
the undulating body.
I forgive the hole
in the leaf
of the apple tree.

I regard again
the fly
squat and braced.

I hover
on the brink
of intervention
like an uncertain god

but the fly
suddenly
strikes:

a single ferocious stab
to the soft side
of the caterpillar
then – gone.

The caterpillar
writhes
on the leaf
in an ecstasy
of wounding.
Its front end is up,
its head
it curls back on itself,
it sways,
screws into a ball,
a kind of dervish dance,
it twists
onto its back,

its russet underside,
its paddling feet.

Then its head
finds the wound

a bubble
of translucent fluid,
its life
leaking out.

What to do?
What to do?

Down from the apple-tree leaf
climbs the caterpillar.

Down onto a branch and along
it goes, pausing to tend its wound.

Down it goes, undulant and resolute
until
                    safe beneath a lower leaf
in the cradle of a bough
it curls to tend its wounded side —

and how does it go, that line

that *every creature shall be to thee
a mirror of life*?

Gwen

gwenu gwenu gwenu gwenu
gwenu gwenu gwenu gwenu . . .
SUPER FURRY ANIMALS

On the night before the little black cat
was due to be put to sleep for the cancer,
she left the room she had chosen to make her home
those last two years, in the house she had slipped into
through the cat flap, a refuge from the hunger
and the toms that kept her womb filled.

She left the room she had found for herself
where all the tastiest food she could eat
was placed daily before her:
milk and biscuits and gourmet tins
that made her sing and shine beneath the hands
that stroked her.

                    She left the utility room
that had become her world, with its washing machine
and freezer and clothes hanging there to air

and visited all the rooms in the house, one by one,
with methodical care.
                    Her people found her
on a kitchen chair in the morning,
her poor mouth dripping down her black fur
but still, her purr sounding out
around the room

and in the vet's surgery
on the treatment table,
she sang to the last
that same tune.

What my riding teacher told me

as I lay there on my back in the paddock,
my breath and me parted, my horse
and me similarly gone from each other
and the shock of planet earth resounding
through my frame, was: you must
remount, you must slip your foot
back into the stirrup, that shiny thing,
and close your legs around the horse
that flipped you out of the saddle.

She was not a tall woman, my riding teacher,
but from ground level, she grew into the sky
like a beanstalk. Her hand was a giantess's
reaching down, my arm floated towards her,
and when she heaved me to my feet, I noticed how
a rattled head feels watching a small woman
striding in tall boots to where the mare nibbled grass,
a small woman seizing the looping reins,
turning towards me, leading the chestnut back
to where I was thinking: this is the woman
who sometimes bends double with period pains
and an errant husband who lays his palm
on the thighs of all the pretty young girls
just long enough for them to know
he is doing more than showing how the thigh muscle
should lie flat against the flap of the saddle
and the legs should relax downwards at the heel.

And I took the reins from her
and slipped my toe into the stirrup
and hauled myself up and onto the back
of the chestnut mare, and rode on.

Bringing in the Horses

In winter, we bring the horses in
at four o'clock. The stables spill
yellow light across the yard. The radio
is on counting shopping days left till Christmas
while we bustle to and from the barn,
filling and tying up nets of hay for the night.

The horses know the routine.
They mill around the gate,
where the mud squelches,
and grow fractious and keen.
We hump brimming water buckets to each stall,
fluff up clean straw beds,
mix oats, bran, barley and treacle into separate feeds,
all warmed with water from the kettle.

Then, with each stable ready,
we slip the gate's bolt
and the horses push through.
We need do little then
but steer the timid,
scold the bossy.

Swinging the half-doors closed behind them,
we secure the latches and then, loose-lipped
and vicarious, lean over the stable doors
to watch the horses settle for the night.
Whatever the weather – still moonlit frost
or hammering hail – we leave the stables
warm and happy and safely gathered in.

Home Turf

1
Flash of face
as the car passes –
it is Iwan,
his hand in a wave.

2
Across the yellowed fields
the chicken factory lies.

3
Grug Fawr, Crug Bach
and Pensarn.

Triangle
of bright sky
behind bare branches.

4
Rubbish bin, half-rusted –
form falling away
to emptiness

5
Up Lovers' Lane –
the sound of a gate
goes clack, clack, clack.

Everything is disappearing.

6
Green-gated cattle pen –
its padlock and chain rattle
in the breeze.

The Twelfth Day of Christmas

Walk the dogs on Aberffraw common, the moon
full and faint in the late afternoon blue-wash sky.
Tonight we'll unwind, from the branch of sycamore, the tinsel,
unhook the red and white wooden angels, the skaters and santas,
unplug the coloured lights that have lit our recent evenings
and pack Christmas away for another year.

Roy says he's seen snowdrops out already,
and here is Lleucu, white feet in the mud,
her tail waving, joyously.

Lleucu

This dog
        balances her tennis ball
on my knee
                and crouches
ready.
            Her pupils flood
her green eyes – life
is acute
        in her.
As for me,
                I am
as dimmed as an old penny.
I take off my glasses
and cast the ball
                upwards.
She catches it
with the effortlessness
of *wu wei*
        and returns it to me
brimming
                with play.

View from Barclodiad y Gawres

It's only cloud
with the light coming through
fiercely
      a great shaft
falling towards Ynys Enlli.

It's only cumulus
sharp-edged by the sun
setting
      behind it.

It's only sunlight
pouring down into the sea
slanted
      towards Ynys Enlli.

The Nature of Light

In that moment she saw
the single shaft of light
split
      into
the myriad things:
fine gold lines
like her own hair
          pulled out
across green space,
long lit hair
combed straight and silken,
each strand
         standing
for the glossy nature
of light –
        and only
that they tremble
and only
      that they are
there for the seeing
and that the spray of beams
seem to seek the heart
and can be followed back
to the flame.

Thursday Morning

(For Mishelle, written during her operation)

You
      are held
in crystal
          light,
the shards
          of quartz
testimony
          to the earth –

rock
      beneath you,
sky above
          and the mystery
of being
          and not-being
      between.

Because the Poet

(For John Powell Ward)

Because of your faith
in language and what
can come through
these marks we make
on white, that can shine
enough to stir our matter;

because of your faith
in the act of coming here
that saves us from mute non-
being, if words can help, because
hold this poem up
to the light and

because all this can, it can
like a butterfly
flap its wings
and a crack can open
and truth (that word)
can run like some honey-
stuff because

coming here
feels real and something
that we may say yes to
against all that is no,
against all that is a raging no,
that is a mouth
devouring

and I am small
against it all

but at least
because of
and faithful to

I come here
like you.

Why I write

To keep myself small
and connected to the silence that supports us all
out of which things come
like poems.

I, like others, suffer
from a swollen condition whereby
the words 'me' and 'my'
cause me to balloon and soon
I'm so full of (hot) air
that I'm floating
above the heads
of the few who
don't do this.

Writing is one of the fine
sharp pinpricks I need,
an instrument I play,
a beautiful thing
for cases of inflation.
I can pierce the membrane
and maybe hiss a bit
but down I go
and it's safe,
doesn't cause too much of a stink.

Too bad if I've let myself go
too high (falling can so bruise the bones
and if you've drifted into the sky, well . . .)
and the bigger the balloon
the louder the bang
as everyone knows –
gas-bags are going off
all over the place
and space is calamitous
with blown-up beings bouncing off each other.

Once punctured however
humour returns
our natural shape,
a (thank you) godsend.

After WCW
(and Peter Finch)

I have eaten
the first loganberry
from the garden.

I'm sorry.
It pulsed such a red
I couldn't resist.

But it was sour.
I spat it out.
So you didn't
miss much.

Dahlia

A single
flowerhead
flames,
as consummate
with the October sun
as Mechtild
with her God:

I am your reflection.
How can I resist
my own true nature?

Waiting for the 11.56 at Llandudno Junction

The world does not ask for belief.
It asks for noticing, attention,
appreciation, and care

JAMES HILLMAN

I

The mallow
                    is always
in bloom here.

My eyes
            greet the mauve-pale
            flowerheads
as old friends.

The Platform 1 sign
is an instrument
the wind
plays: *The Hinge's Complaint.*

A gull wing-beats
            across the track
and pigeons roost
in the wrought-iron roof beams
or waddle along the platform
picking at dropped bits.

II

I have been reading
about the possibilities
                    of writing
a twenty-first-century religious poem:

to *reach beyond this or that*
religious doctrine into areas of experience
perennially essential –

into my clearing, the world comes
with its bits of platform paraphernalia:
wet train tickets and cigarette stumps.

III

This is what I want: *to make the most of being alive.*

IV

Some red flower
– a dog rose –
                    flames
behind the pampas grass:
it and I and a grey sky.

V

A man in falling-down jeans
pushes a child in a pram
onto the platform.

The child is saying 'train'
and the man says 'train' and
we on the platform
follow his finger down the track –

I am back with *the mystery of things*
and spontaneous love.

VI

Waiting for the train
is waiting for the poem is
tracking the details

which everywhere
          seem to seek
witness.

VII

A true poem is not valued as
statement
                    cannot be reduced
to paraphrase.

VIII

We are all together in this.

IX

We rustle like birds
as we gather ourselves
for the onward journey,
folding up our books
          and thoughts.
As the train pulls in,
                    the child
and the man
          clap their hands –

I take the vast outside
into myself.

Avalokiteśvara on the day his Great Compassion was born

It was this morning it happened,
being full
                    of cold and love and sorrow.

Felt like a great welling up.

A pressure

                    in the heart centre.

I thought *oh oh*

here it comes (not being sure at that point
what *it* was).

In the mirror
my face shone red
and everything was flowing
as is the way with colds, love and sorrow.

That feeling in my chest,
                    it was
like waters rising
against a dam
like a wringing out
of everything I am −

my eyes were waterfalling,
my nose running great streams
along my throat, its banks of thistledown

and then the shivers began
and my head split

and finally it was the sight of a wren
on a fennel stalk
that did it.

Getting down off the fence

I am
        getting down
off the fence.

It is a slow
        arduous business.

The fence has a solid appearance
and is higher from the ground
than expected.

Also
        it has creeping stuff
growing through it
that clutches at you.

If you pause for a moment,
the rampant tendrils
bind you again to the fence
and wrap you up in leafage
till you've lost your view.

That's when you begin to doubt
the ground.

You've lost sight of it.

Maybe it's not to be found at all.

Unlike the familiarity of the fence
and the creeper, that you cling to.

I will not manage
to get both feet on the ground
without the scraping off

of skin, some tattering
to my garments.

I can already see
the trail of the me
I am leaving behind:

it's a bit like slug spoor.

Playing with the Boys

Be like John Wayne, this is best.
Make guns out of Lego
and be a Green Beret.

Make the noises: peow! peow!
Learn to crawl in the sand
and ignore where it goes.

It is necessary to stay dead
once shot: no laughing.

Lob the tennis ball
over the wall, then
flat on the floor.

Splatter the enemy with spit
from your machine-gun stick
and, one morning, say:

*Can we take a break, and play
something else?*

Magda's Song

No rest, we walk on in silence.
But for the weeping
and the whimpers of the children,
there are no words and my name is lost.

My husband of fifty-two years —
an old man, his veins hardening
and his back weakened from a life of work —
they took, tore from me though I fell to my knees
and beggingly clutched at the legs of men
who held our lives at gunpoint.
What use is he, an old man like him?
No threat to your regime!
But my words were kicked to the door
and out into the mud. See, I have the bruises
though they are numb.

Some of the men they left undead — few —
whose hands still fluttered like shot birds
who think they may yet fly. The rest
they made cattle of, carted off
and oh, that ripped last look he gave me,
my husband of fifty-two years.

Soon we will reach the border
and though I pray with each step I take
for these young ones, these babes,
these widow girls and broken mothers,
for myself, I have nothing to ask.
My feet stumble forwards following
my townsfolk to some sanctuary (they say)
getting away with life still somehow breathing us.
But my soul is not in this nameless shell —
it has spilled out. It is back with the whining dogs,
and the flies already feeding off the dead wounds
of my husband, of fifty-two years.

Autobiography 1

September 1964/March 2003

When I was five,
my father drove us
from Portsmouth to Qatar
in his new Jaguar

and what I remember
was the drive across the desert of Iraq
and a Land Rover full of the Sheikh's men

pulling us out of the sand
again and again,

returning for us,
feeding us,
and leading us
to Baghdad.

Tonight, in Wales,
the TV-screen shows that place ablaze
as shock-and-awe destruction
sinks in
            and I can only think
of that bright sun on my young head
and the feeling I couldn't then name
of being part of a circle in the sand, sharing rice.

Rant of the Buckled Feet

*Free circulation of information is essential
to health and survival*

JOANNA MACY

I

We can no longer
            stand you.
We cannot bear
            your importunate weight.
You are too top-heavy
                    high up there
in your penthouse suite.
You have made us
                    unsteady.

The tower
            sways,
threatens to fall,
and you, your un-listening ears,
don't notice at all.

You have lost our trust.

The system is close to collapse.

II

You are
            filled
with your own
            noise   so full
of thoughts
            in their grooves,
mission control high up there,

                    head
so full
        in the clouds.
And we,
        way down here, weighed down,
weighted down,
                are carrying
                you,
        weight-bearing
(not bearing
                you)
not bearing
                (no longer bearing)
today must bare
                ourselves
to you
        as we are: bone-aching,
pain getting through.

Our pain –
                yes –
is yours.

It is true.

Where is the line
that separates us from you?

III

The system flounders in fog.

It's the old story of the king in his court
drowning out the body's needs
with the machine tick-tock
of noise, planes, plans,
propositions, polemical –

anything to keep silence at bay

and what the silence might say.

IV

So we fire
arrows.

Primitive weaponry
against your high technology
but still effective.

Still effective
as you can see.

They penetrate
your inner sanctum,
burst through
your hard wall
of defence.

V

We are every ass, every worn, weary,
broken, tethered thing,
                                    every creature,
every part of the whole

over-ruled, over-looked, over-ridden,
walked on, tested on, cast-out thing.

VI

The rune says:
that which is ignored
wreaks havoc –

the system
is close to collapse.

VII

You have not yet descended
to be among us,

climbed down
the necessary steps
to realise yourself
as each subterranean cell
each crevice where life hangs dearly.

You and your elite institutions
cocoon against us,
but all the fortresses in the world
are whimsy;
                    all the affluent distractions
cannot save your skin.

But your skin (precious skin)
can bring your face to face

                              its
                              self
as it is:

unfathomable

irreducible

to facts –

Dearest you are in hell again

Dearest, you are in hell again.
Wishing to pull you out, I reach my hand
down through the smoking ice and vacant tundra
to where you are set,
and, being so brittle, you snap
at the elbow.

Your forearm, thawing
up here in the spring balm
is a beginning. Already, its palm
is opening. Peering down,
the rest of you, still in your pit,
must be returned for, though I fear the descent.
I must keep my wits
for the fiend has got you
frozen in his grip.

This is a cold world.
Vast tract of nothing.
In paralysis, you have whitened.
I could snap off your nose – you'd not feel it.
A note in your hand won't come free,
your fingers clenched around it.
A fireman's lift? But the risk is fracture:
you are like glass, you could shatter.

My own arms, then, my own body
around you, and a long wait of silence,
breath at your nostrils faint. The light here
is stark, without source. Not polar,
not anywhere you'd know. And no
to and fro, seasons, cycles, arrows of time –
the fiend has made you believe
the *immôbilis*.

I practise what to say should I too be taken.
I rehearse mantras of protection.

The 'C' Snag

(For Gav)

The silver-service waiter occasioned
an elegant bend at the waist, one forearm
folded behind his immaculate back.

Would any sweets be required? he inclined,
directing the question at you, of course:
head of the table and looking the part.

What you meant to say was: *Could we
see the menu please*, but the 'C' snagged
like a fish bone, caught in your throat.

C . . . C . . . C . . . you said, fixing the waiter
a fish-eye stare, as if he were reeling you in on a hook.
C . . . C . . . C . . . you said, while the waiter

bowed lower, his eyebrows raised in an effort
of encouragement, his eyes locked on yours
and yours on his, as if in a desperate love affair.

Around us, other tables hovered inches off the floor.
Knives and forks and even spoons hung in the haute air.
All clatter ceased. *C . . . C . . . C . . .* you beseeched.

C . . . C . . . C . . . you creaked.

Then it came, on a breaker of breath:
Couldweseethemenuplease? The whole room breathed.
Certainly Sir, the waiter said, sprung free.

Owen Huw's Winter Holiday

(For Owen Huw)

It was in Austria that it happened.
We went up the mountain on a lift.
Everything sparkled in the morning sun –
the snow, the trees – like a yuletide scene.
Halfway up, a woman called to the leader
could he stop the lift, please. She needed to pee.
A nice-looking woman in a green snowsuit,
eyebrows angling *sorry*.

He had to walkie-talkie to the top
but the whole party slowed then stopped
on the mountainside, our feet dangling
off the ground. The leader (Hans)
helped the woman down and gestured to some trees
and we, politely, turned our heads away
as she slithered there on her skis.
We shifted in our seats and blew our noses
and agreed that a mug of grog would be good.

Then a small squeal had all our attention.
The whole party turned in one direction
as the woman, in squatting position, slid
out of the trees, her green ski-suit
gathered round her knees
and a trail bright in the snow
as she picked up speed.

Autobiography 2

One bright star
in an indigo sky.

'Der's a tar up der' –
first words I heard
myself saying.

Twinkly star
alone and brave
against all that
swallowing night.

This star is a planet –
Venus or Mars?

Twinkle twinkle ickle tar –

sky's darkness is almost complete.

Little diamond stud
standing for *light*
and for that which *cuts*,

how I wonder
how I could have been,
how that little songster in a cot
looking up, pointing her ickle finger
to maybe dis tar
was me.

What I was,
what I am,
what I will be –

who else
is writing a poem
about this star
at this moment?

Velvety night,
the star a pinprick
letting through light.

Torn Xmas Card

Was it Jehovah or the torn Christmas card?
Mum, hissing at Dad, behind the kitchen door.
She is a farmyard goose gone wild, a more
than beak, a wafting wing-span yards
wide. But why? His sister has come to stay
with her orange book. The cover says:
Paradise Lost to Paradise Regained,
a picture book of the world in flames.

It was end of term. I went
straight to Aunty Toss's room, to present
her with the card I'd made in art:
a snow scene and a big red heart.
She tore it up. Christmas was a lie.
A note in the kitchen: 'She goes, or I fly.'

Because I can't tell you to your face

Sometimes, my dearest one,
you talk so much that I age
before your intent gaze
and you do not notice

my shifting, sighing signals
of distress. I am too weak
or kind. I mind hurting you,
so I allow myself to sit

all hour silent. Sometimes
I drift away and hear you
as backdrop, but your fixed
eye pins me back into present.

Really, there's no getting away
other than with the honesty
I haven't got for you. I am
grey mouse, I am owl's prey.

I want you wise, owl.
I want a two-way say.
When you have finished,
I break in the bathroom,

gnash teeth at the mirror,
sob myself hot until I love
you again. Toilet paper
blots away the pain.

The boy who hated stew

My father is pleased with himself
for finishing his meal. He shows
us his clean plate: nothing
much left on that.

My father would rather live
on antacid tablets than suffer the ignominy
of leaving food.
                    When he was seven
his own father sat with him a whole
two hours until he – the boy who hated stew –
finished the last of it. The clock ticked loud
in that Somerset kitchen one hundred
and twenty minutes. Mutton fat
whitened on the plate. Boiled potato
chilled to the temperature of the room.
His father, with his hands on the table top,
straight-backed in the girdle he wore
for the shrapnel lodged in his spine
from the Great War, sat the boy out.
Each forkful taken lodged the lesson
deeper: eat what you're given
and *don't waste food*.

My father is proud to be his father's son.
He lives his lesson daily
each clean plate a victory.

Letter to the Welsh Pony and Cob Society

'To whom it may concern. This is to inform you
that Mr. R.M. Strongetharm, life member . . . '

        and I pause, tracing your name along the line,
        seeing your hand again in mine at the bedside,
        remembering your signature, the right-sloping
        right-handed writing

'that Mr Robert Malcolm . . .'

        your first name that of your father,
        your second that of your father's brother
        (the policeman uncle you thought was a crook),
        Malcolm, the name of your second son, third child
        (three of us in all) my need to place you and us
        in time, link us up, join the dots, follow the lines
        backwards, outwards, inwards, forwards

'Strongetharm . . .'

        my maiden name, the one that people asked about:
        'oh that's a strange/interesting/unique/unusual/
        Nordic?/Northern? name.'
        Like Strong in th'arm, said in a Yorkshire accent.

'Life member . . .'

        Member of life, *as was*.
        The 'M' removed to leave 'ember'
        (and Mum, with a cry, rising from her seat
        reaching for where the curtains swung
        round the coffin to make the exit discreet)

'. . . has now passed away. His life membership,
therefore, has ceased.'

        Yours. Faithfully. Daughter. Fiona.

Thirtieth of December

(For Lisa and Mark)

We are the cousins around the table
on the night of Aunty Pat's funeral.
We share kettle crisps and reminisce,
filling in the gaps of our collective story.
We are not often together. Funerals
and weddings remind us of our mutual
origins. The bottle of port is emptying
and the sing-songing of the mobile phone
doesn't distract, but when you come back,
you are sober. 'Not more bad news?'
Your friends are in Phuket. They were
on the beach on Boxing Day, their daughter
sucked away. Her swallowed scream
deafens them daily as they wait for the DNA
report that will wipe her off the missing list.

Tomorrow night, there will only be candles lit
in Phuket, and we are silenced now,
death too big around our table.

Speaking as a Familiar

(I.M. Mrs Kitty Jones)

And so you have gone to him
who has been curled like a cat,
these last months, against your legs,
refusing to budge.

Your warmth held him
in that zone between
here and *there*:

going over was not to be done
without you and, in sensing his pull,
you began to give up your colour.

And when I last saw you,
we stood in your cold kitchen,
our hands in each other's,
eyes damp from repeating the past:
'you will always be his *Miss Fiona*'.

Out of respect, I wrote each year
for years: *Nadolig Llawen, Mr and Mrs Jones*.
But today, Kitty, I will speak
personally (moving from *chi* to *ti*):

I hope his face was there
as you broke through,
that you flew off *together*

into that oblique horizon.

Sunday Afternoon

At the root of Being there's not one witheredness.
The heartwood is safe.

WALDO WILLIAMS/TONY CONRAN

The winter sun streams across the page
and the north wind that blew on Friday
has dropped.

It blew your candle out

and, this morning, we sat with the shock
of your afterwards.

But the space that you now are
is not a darkness.

You were light this morning,
a bright spot in every memory
and through our sadness, we glimpsed
your safekeeping.

In memory of Robert Wales, our Friend.
For Holyhead Meeting.

After Oz's funeral

*Boneddigion a boneddigesau,
a fyddwch mor garedig â chymryd
eich amser. Mae tragwyddoldeb ar fin dechra.**

(For Dewi Evans)

I stand in the bedroom, gloves and coat
on the bed and rain falling
against the window. We were all there
to see him off (*sing on, friend*).

Out in the garden, everything drips
a winter green – death's season,
when what was given is taken
back to the earth.

Out there, among the mossy sycamores,
sudden sun strikes through the slaty cloud.
There is the folksy sunflower we painted on the shed front.
There is the weather cockerel, pointing west.
These are the things of our life, lit for a moment,
and who can say how many moments will make up a lifetime?

Sunshine and showers – they forecast this.
Some things you can predict. Others are the chancy
twists and turns of circumstance.

Like this rainbow: sudden brilliance
arching over the rooftops of Rehoboth,
a gift of colour and another
of life's miracles –

and Oz: *this one's for you!*

---

* Epigraph translation: 'Ladies and gentlemen, would you be so kind as to take
your time. Eternity is about to begin'.

Going gentle

The purest
step across that frontier
without struggle.

You offered
only trust

and yielded —

left wisdom
glowing
in your jewelled eyes
like the Buddha himself.

One use of space is
For speaking across, another
To deepen silence

Jeremy Hooker

Y rhwng.
Ar y naill law a'r llall.

Aled Jones Williams

Acknowledgements

Various poems in this collection were published previously in the following magazines and journals, so thanks are due to the editors of: *Scintilla, Fire, Big Bridge, New Welsh Review, Obsessed with Pipework, Skald, Orbis, Red Poets.*

Notes

page v Oliver, Mary *Long Life: Essays and Other Writings* (Da Capo Press, 2004).

p. 9 'Walk' was commended in *Scintilla 2002* competition.

p. 10 'Door' was commended in *Scintilla 2004* competition and is also included in the anthology *Into the Further Reaches* ed. Jay Ramsay (P S Avalon, 2007).

p. 11 'winter's harbinger' is quoted from 'Breath Sentences' in Jeremy Hilton's *Slipstream* (Ripostes, 2003).

p. 12 Epigraph: 'Yeah is what we had' on *Sumday* by Grandaddy (V2 Records, CD).

p. 13 Epigraph: Suzy Gablik about artist Dominique Mazeaud in *The Reenchantment of Art* (Thames & Hudson, 2002).

p. 23 Final quotation: Thomas à Kempis. This poem won third prize in the *Scintilla 2006* competition.

p. 24 Epigraph from 'Pam V' by Super Furry Animals, *Moog Droog* (Ankst, CD062).

p. 32 This is set in a sonic art piece entitled *The Dress* by composer Rob Godman.

p. 33 The line 'hold this poem up to the light' is from the poem 'From a Phrase by Janet Montefiore' by John Powell Ward in *A Certain Marvellous Thing* (Seren, 1993). 'Because the Poet' is included in the anthology *Into the Further Reaches*.

p. 38 Work by Mechtild of Magdeburg can be found in Hirshfield, J. (ed.) *Women in Praise of the Sacred* (HarperPerennial, 1995).

p. 39–41 Epigraph: Hillman, J. quoted in *The Reenchantment of Art*. Quotations are taken from *Is a religious poem possible in the 21st century* (Flarestack, 2004). II and VII: Anne Cluysenaar. III and V: Henry Shukman. IX: a paraphrase of a line by Billy Collins quoted by David Healey.

p. 42 Avalokiteśvara is a Bodhisattva of compassion in the Buddhist tradition.

p. 49 Epigraph: quoted in Macy, Joanna and Young Brown, Molly *Coming Back to Life* (New Society Publishers, 1998).

p. 63 '*Nadolig Llawen*' means 'Merry Christmas'; '*chi* to *ti*' indicates the move from the formal to the familiar 'you'.

p. 64 Epigraph: Williams, Waldo/Conran, Tony (trans.) *The Peacemakers* (Gomer, 1997).

p. 65 Epigraph: lyrics by Oz Wright in 'Edward Yn Hedfan' by Rheinallt H. Rowlands, *Rheinallt III* (Ankstmusik, CD 095).

p. 67 Hooker, Jeremy from 'Steps' in *Their Silence a Language* (Enitharmon Press, 1993); Williams, Aled Jones *Oerfel Gaeaf Duw* (Gwasg Pantycelyn, 2002). Translation: 'The between. On the one hand and the other'.